Parts Of The Sch

PART 1

Finding Scholarships

That You're More Likely to Win

PART 2

Optimization x Organization

Scholarship List and Templates

PART 3

Constructing Your Essay

Winning Excerpts
What to Write

PART 4

Filling Out The Application

Free Online Resources
Reference Letters

Disclaimer

The knowledge I have acquired about scholarships comes with years of experience and research. With that in mind, the money I get from selling this book partially goes towards certain educational initiatives/programs aimed towards increasing accessibility to higher education. And one of which includes creating a scholarship fund, so to award students such as yourself.

So please do not redistribute or plagiarize this.

Table of Contents

PART 2 | Optimization x Organization

PART 3 | Constructing Your Essay

PART 4 | Filling Out The Application

CARLYNN GREENE

WWW.SCHOLARSHIP-GURU.COM

Dedication

This book is dedicated to all the students, mentors, educators, counselors, coaches, and parents of students responsible for funding their education or encouraging them to pursue their education.

In the words of the late Nelson Mandela —

"Education is the most powerful weapon which you can use to change the world."

And my job with this book and all of what I do to help others is to make sure that education is more accessible to **you**.

View **below** some of those who **won** with *The Scholarship Algorithm* **book** and **program:**

https://bit.ly/SGprogramxbook

Preface

During my high school senior year, I won a lot of scholarships and years later, I am still winning — **30 scholarships**, for a total of **$125,000**. On top of that, I have helped students in the U.S. and globally win collectively **millions in scholarships** — from as close as Arizona to as far as Indonesia and South Sudan. And note that this number only accounts for those who have personally told me that they won. I imagine that the total is **actually 5x more.**

College is expensive, and it gets more and more expensive every single year. And of course, it doesn't help that the minimum wage and average household incomes haven't seen much of a rise, which makes it even harder for people to afford college.

Not enough people know what it takes to win scholarships. There's a lot of misinformation out there, as well as tips that are too generalized, outdated, or vague in helping a student with the process. And that is why I wrote this book. This book serves as a means to bridge the gap — and I hope it helps you win!

"I won $85,000 in scholarships from Amazon, FOSSI and AFCEA after buying your book." - Tolulope Oluyadi, Howard University

"I'm honored to have been selected as a recipient of the Dr. Pepper Tuition Giveaway ($100,000) in a pool of over 111,000 applicants. Your videos, advice, book, and motivation works -- thanks a ton!" - Chris Karr, Texas A&M Corpus Christi

"After reading your book, I have been able to earn a $10,000 scholarship and a $5,000 scholarship per year and an additional $9,500 scholarship per year from Penn State ($68,000 total)." - Michael Garza, Pennsylvania State University

Why I started helping others:

What started me on this journey of helping others with scholarships was my mother. My senior year of high school, I won a scholarship from a hospital I had been volunteering at for years. I was asleep in my room and I woke up to my mother at the side of my bed, on her knees, crying, shaking, and thanking God over and over again. She was holding the award letter for the scholarship that I won.

That was when I realized that the knowledge I have obtained about scholarships shouldn't be kept to myself. From there on out, I had a responsibility to help not only other students but also the parents because so many times parents are the ones who bear the financial burden of paying for their education.

My reaction the first time someone told me they won:

The first time someone told me they won a scholarship was in 2017 via email. Not only was this student the first one to tell me they won, but they were also not from the U.S. — they were from the D.R. Congo, studying in Ghana on a **full-ride**. And just recently, another student — this time one who happens to be a refugee from South Sudan — was awarded a **full-ride** to study in Egypt.

Upon reading these messages, I cried for a good ten minutes. It literally felt like an out-of-body experience. I couldn't believe that my advice/words that I had filmed in my parents' bedroom, with a cheap/used camera, and amateur video editing skills — were able to reach across the ocean. That was when I knew that what I was doing — was *groundbreaking*.

Legitimacy and credibility:

Whenever I promote what I do, most of the time I receive positive feedback. However, there are also those who see what I do and automatically assume that it is a "scam" or "not legit."

Nowhere have I ever said that with my advice a student is "100 percent guaranteed" to receive a scholarship. If I were to say that, then yes, that would be dishonest. What I can say instead is that with my advice you will be much more likely to win because you will be seeing exactly how my mind works as far as writing effective scholarships essays and research techniques that have not only secured me scholarship money, but even more for others across the globe.

In addition to this, I am a journalist, and being in journalism is heavily dependent on research, writing skills, and above all else, transparency and legitimacy. If I were scamming people that would literally ruin my career which is based on credibility. I'm just trying to make higher education more accessible.

Furthermore my work has been nationally recognized which is apparent from receiving a **$15,000 grant** from LinkedIn, a **$50,000 grant** from TikTok/MACRO, and in 2020 I won the ADCOLOR **TikTok Creator Award** for my scholarship content that promotes diversity/inclusion.

If you would like to learn more about who I have helped win so far and even view multiple published news stories about what I do, then view the two links below.

- **Winner testimonies:** https://bit.ly/SGscholarshipwinners
- **News/press coverage:** https://bit.ly/sgurunews

Acknowledgments

I would like to thank:

My parents and all their support towards my education.

My mentor, Chase, and her non-profit, *Coach The Youth*, for giving me my first-ever laptop — this was the laptop I used to find/apply for scholarships during my senior year of high school.

My counselor from high school, Mr. Fitz, who would often encourage and notify me about scholarships.

My professors, Dr. McElroy and Dr. Fellows, and my classmate, Jasmine, who wrote my letters of recommendation that aided in awarding me several scholarships. Also, I want to thank them for being the ones responsible for further improving my writing skills and work ethic.

The University of North Texas and the Mayborn School of Journalism for all the exposure and opportunities afforded to me through this mission of mine.

All the scholarship committees who have ever awarded me.

And of course — my YouTube subscribers, TikTok followers, clients, and those who purchased the book, such as yourself! Thank you.

Introduction

From this book, you will be equipped with resources and techniques I have used to land back-to-back scholarships.

A lot of the advice seen in this book has yet to be reiterated elsewhere from other existing blogs, scholarship books, videos — and most of the content has yet to be disclosed on my YouTube channel, ESP Daniella. If you would like an even more in-depth learning experience on how to win scholarships, consider enrolling in my online course. You will be 5x more likely to win with the entire four-part book, yet 10x more likely to win scholarships learning from the course which has the option of being bundled in with my services.

The scholarship process is very tedious and can be quite time-consuming and stressful depending on the demands of certain applications. However, you must stay encouraged and you must keep applying. Think of it as a part-time job that will pay you sooner or later.

I've applied for well over 100 scholarships from the summer of 2016 to the summer of 2021. From that, I saw more rejection than anything. But instead of thinking I couldn't win because there were others more qualified or smarter, I learned from my mistakes, analyzed what I could do to make my application stronger and more convincing, and once I did that, I finally was able to decode what I like to call, "The Scholarship Algorithm."

So, just know that you may be in for the long-run for this entire process — or perhaps you can win enough scholarships from the beginning. Either way, stay encouraged, don't give up, and be consistent! I was for five years, and I must say that the hard work paid off. I just graduated from the University of North Texas with my B.A. in Broadcast Journalism, magna cum laude, **debt-free! Additionally,** I am currently pursuing my master's in public relations, yet again, **debt-free.**

However, my journey doesn't stop there.

Outside of graduate school, I was able to secure a summer internship with Disney/ABC News working at the national level. Also, I want to note that the process of securing jobs and internships is very similar to winning scholarships. So, this book can also be resourceful when it comes to applying for those opportunities as well.

WWW.SCHOLARSHIP-GURU.COM

Scholarships Today

Most scholarships are catered to high school seniors who will be incoming freshmen.

The reason for this is in a way quite strategic. Schools get enrollment numbers up by awarding money to primarily incoming students, but once they are in, there are fewer scholarships and overall funding available for current college students.

However, it is still possible for you to win scholarships as a current college student and as a high schooler. You just have to decode the algorithm — like I did!

Here is the breakdown of the scholarships I won:

I won about 14 scholarships during my senior year of high school.

However, only 10 of those could be applied to my education.

Then when I started back applying in my junior/senior year of college, I won 12 scholarships.

And most recently, I won four scholarships for graduate school — one of which happens to be a $10,000 award from NBC.

To see the full list of the 30 scholarships I have won, go to this link here: http://bit.ly/2JDdCCl.

Important note: Throughout the book, several links will be mentioned redirecting to scholarships, resources, templates etc. If you are reading this as a physical copy of the book, rather than typing in each individual URL link, make sure to refer to **pg. 86 of services/products** to access the **master link and QR code** to scan!

What It Takes To Win Scholarships
S.C.O.P.E

Strategy

This involves mastering indirect-persuasive writing and finding scholarships that you not only meet the criteria but also have an edge. The book will explain what I mean by it being 'indirect'.

Competitiveness

There are going to be people applying who are more qualified or smarter. Even so, figure out what makes you stand out.

Organization

If you're not organized, it will take you longer to complete applications, and you might even miss deadlines!

Positivity

Going into the process with the right attitude will take you far. You'll work more efficiently and produce better results.

Endurance

You're going to face rejection. It might be discouraging but keep applying! Your hard work will pay off sooner or later.

Part 1

Finding Scholarships

That You're More Likely To Win

Do Not Apply For + Scholarship Scams

Typically, I would advise to stay away from applying for **too many** sponsored scholarships from popular scholarship sites. By this, I mean ones where that particular site is the one funding it themselves, **or** an external scholarship that the site lists as an ad.

They may be legit — but since these are on the most popular / most used sites, you are less likely to win because they get more exposure and so more students are applying. The eligibility pool is typically too broad, meaning just about anyone can apply, which makes it more competitive — it's like trying to win the lottery!

There are also what are referred to as scholarship sweepstakes. Sometimes they might also be labeled as drawings or raffles, meaning selected at random.

However, it is okay to use these sites as search engines for scholarships that are not funded by the sites, but instead just listed there. But still, don't be overly dependent on them — **do outside research!**

Also on that note, if a scholarship is labeled as "easy" more times than none it is in fact **not easy.** Just think about it — people gravitate towards something that doesn't take much effort but avoids things that require more time. So in reality a scholarship that requires more paperwork to fill out is arguably easier to get as opposed to a two to five-minute application.

If a scholarship asks for your social security number — during the application phase — most of the time I would advise NOT to apply. There are quite a few scholarship SCAMS out there. However, I have won two scholarships that asked for my social security number, but only AFTER I was awarded. So, in order to determine the legitimacy of a scholarship asking for this information, make sure you do a background check on them and get someone's else opinion (such as from an educator or a parent). For instance, a scholarship I won that required this info was from the Society of Professional Journalists which is one of the most accredited organizations for those working in media, so I knew it was coming from a legitimate source.

Stray away from only applying for scholarships that require no essay — the reason being? The essay is where you will be able to tell in more detail **who** you are and **why** you deserve the award. Without it, your application is nothing more than a number and they'll only judge you based on test scores, GPA, class ranking, and so on. Again, it's like entering sweepstakes or lotteries.

However — sometimes it is okay to apply for these such as if the competitive pool is narrowed down by one if not multiple elements such as your:

- Demographic (race, ethnicity, gender, sexuality)
- City/region/state/school district
- Major/study concentration

Some additional exceptions would be if the application instead requires your:

- Resume and/or cover letter
- Portfolio of your work
- Video submission of yourself and/or your work

If a scholarship's site is bombarded with ads all over the place, typically that also is a red flag that it is probably not legit. Here are some signs to **spot a legit scholarship** so that you **don't get scammed.** If they have a website, typically it should show:

- Their contact info.
- A modern website that has been updated fairly recently.
- Faces of those behind the scholarship and/or those who won previously.
- Other community projects they have worked on.

If you are **still unsure** whether or not a scholarship is legit or not, try and **get a second opinion** from someone such as an educator, a financial aid office worker, or even someone you know who has experience with winning scholarships.

Finding scholarships that you are not only eligible for but also have a good shot at winning is already hard enough as it is. The better you can identify which scholarships you shouldn't apply for, the less you will be wasting your time. The last thing you want is to have spam emails and phone calls following you years after the fact because you filled out a scholarship that wasn't legit.

I say this because to this day I have to experience these types of calls and emails because I was not educated before on what to look for with scholarship scams. **So don't repeat my mistakes.**

Looking back, a lot of the scholarships I applied for I probably shouldn't have. I didn't already have the knowledge that I do now about what **not to do** and what I **should do** to start seeing faster results.

That's why I made sure to start off this book with the very first chapter covering which ones you shouldn't focus your energy on. Some may in fact be legit — but they shouldn't be your focus. Many people focus on these types of scholarships starting off, then they wonder why they never win and end up giving up.

Approved Scholarship Sites

goingmerry.com/

scholarships.com

bold.org

jlvcollegecounseling.com/scholarships/

bigfuture.collegeboard.org/scholarship-search

collegescholarships.com/scholarships/search

salliemae.com

finaid.org/scholarships/

Again, you can still use search engines scholarship sites (such as the ones mentioned above) as well as more popular ones like Unigo, Niche, Fastweb, Scholarship Owl etc.

However, only applying for their sponsored / sweepstakes scholarships or just ones in general that are nationally competitive and very broad with eligibility is like trying to win the lottery! When I started my scholarship process, I was too focused on only applying for these and never won. The same has been the case for most of those I've worked with.

However, there have been **exceptions** to this from students I have helped win (who studied this book). For instance, a student won the $100,000 scholarship from **Dr. Pepper,** the $5,000 award from **Taco Bell,** and another student ended up winning the **Amazon** Future Engineer $40,000 award.

Scholarship To Apply For | Least To Most Competitive

LOCAL NICHE-BASED – meaning scholarships that are local (by organizations, foundations, greek life, associations, local businesses, non-profits, etc.) and are for certain majors/studies, demographics etc.

LOCAL – (city, county, region-level) scholarships of where just about anyone in that area can apply.

UNIVERSITY – those offered by your overall university and those specific to the school/department of your major/study concentration. The more schools you apply for, the more financial options you will have to compare which school offers you the most money relative to their annual cost of attendance.

- **Example:** One particular student told me that she was able to win over $459,000 in scholarships after using my advice. Most of the scholarships she won were for incoming college freshmen to the schools she applied to. (You can view her testimonial and others here: https://bit.ly/SGscholarshipwinners

STATE NICHE-BASED – those offered to state residents/those studying in the state but are specific to major/demographic.

- **Example:** The Texas-based journalism scholarships I got.

NATIONAL NICHE-BASED – scholarships that are open to any citizen (or with a student visa), but are very specific with eligibility, such as regarding your major, demographic etc.

- **Example:** Mine from the Black Congressional Caucus.

5

Apply For Smaller Scholarships

It may be tempting to only apply for scholarships that are in the five-figure and up range ($10,000+) but you will honestly have a better chance at winning scholarships in the $500 to $5,000 range, especially $1,000 scholarships.

Generally, this rule is true:

- The **bigger** the scholarship reward, the **more** competitive.
- The **smaller** the scholarship reward, the **less** competitive.

Just as how I mentioned earlier that people prefer to apply for scholarships that are labeled as "easy" — which in turn makes them harder to get — the same is seen with the amount of money given. Let's say I tell people to form two lines. One line for if they want $1,000 and another if they want $10,000. Now, which line do you think they will neglect vs. gravitate towards?

Bigger scholarships (like those $10,000+) are typically awarded to incoming students — such as high school seniors going to college, or college seniors going to graduate school.

As a current college student, there is less money that goes around and fewer scholarships. **However,** as a current college student, it is still possible for you to win! I was able to win 11 scholarships during my college junior/senior year. The smallest amount was $1,000 — the largest was $6,000. It adds up!

Also — check your school email and type in 'scholarship' or even 'award' in the search box. A lot of the scholarships I applied for (and won) were external which my school notified me about.

6

How To Get A "Full-Ride"

Have you ever heard those stories of students receiving hundreds of thousands if not millions in scholarship money? Well, more than likely they were applying to a lot of different schools and not just two or three.

For instance, the student that I mentioned earlier who won over $459,000 in scholarships. She was accepted into 36 different universities (32 of which were historically black universities/ colleges) and one of those schools gave her a full-ride. If you are still in high school or someone looking to start their undergraduate, graduate school etc., ... **this is your best bet** at getting a full-ride and as much scholarship money as possible!

Important: Apply as early as the summer before your senior year of high school. Try to get familiar with the scholarship and school admissions process beforehand so that you as soon as possible what you are doing right and wrong with your process. Also, note when each school you are interested in has **priority deadlines**. Individually go to their official websites and find this information. Then from there, mark these dates on your **digital calendar** so that you receive sound notifications or email reminders so that you stay on top of deadlines!

From what I have seen, most full-rides and larger scholarships have deadlines ranging from September to early January. Also, if you are still in high school — listen to your parents when they say that you "need to study for tests" (such as the ACT/ SAT). Universities give out more scholarship money according to test scores, ranking, GPA etc. Additionally, quite a few scholarships open up eligibility depending on these stats as well.

Graduate School & Ph.D. Scholarships

Your best bet as a graduate or doctoral student to find external scholarships are through professional organizations. For instance, let's say that you are trying to get your master's degree in nursing. If that's the case, you would want to go to this site here: https://nurse.org/orgs.shtml. From there, you would look at not only the nursing organizations at the national level, but also those listed under the "state" tab because you would be more likely to win those.

To find a lot of professional organizations all within the same area for various career/study concentrations, then please refer to this link here:

- jobstars.com/professional-associations-organizations/

Also, here is a list of international professional organizations:

- en.wikipedia.org/wiki/List_of_international_professional_associations

I encourage you to use CTRL-F or COMM-F on your computer to quickly navigate what you are looking for.

Sallie Mae has a database specifically for graduate school scholarships. This is great because most search engines are very broad and barely show ones that are specifically for grad students. There's also **ProFellow** that will give you 1,000+ fully funded Ph.D. and master's programs both in the U.S. and abroad that are organized by study concentration. Overall, this is an excellent source to learn how to win such awards and there is even an online course provided. Use this link to refer to both resources: https://adobe.ly/3FFI7zh

Look For "Intersectionality Scholarships"

By "intersectionality scholarships" I mean researching based on your identity that can narrow down your search results. For example, in your search engine say something like:

- Asian immigrant/non-U.S. citizen, Latinx LGBTQ, etc.

This will really narrow down scholarships for you and who would be qualified to apply for them, making it less competitive. The same can be said for using a combo of underrepresented status x (classification/grade level, state/city, major, GPA etc).

- **Example:** Black woman Texas scholarships

The more keywords/combinations of those keywords you use as they relate to your identity (by doing separate Google searches each time), the more optimized your search results will be! Download and edit the Q&A below to make your scholarship search process faster: https://bit.ly/2YfU8aU

Also, you can use synonyms or certain keywords relating to your major/study concentration. For example, since I am majoring in broadcast journalism my list would be:

- Media/media arts, communications, TV, video, press etc,.

You can do the same technique with your demographic/location. Then from there, combine those elements:

- **Example:** Black women Texas media scholarships

When I typed this in Google, I was able to narrow down, find and win a scholarship from **Floyd Mayweather's foundation.**

9

Scholarships Based On Major

Think of your major or your intended major if undecided. Now, as mentioned earlier, take the name of your major — plus other words related to your major — and Google/research structures relating to that to create your scholarship list.

Professional organizations such as:

- Foundations
- Associations
- Societies
- Clubs

For instance, some of the scholarships I won were from; the Broadcast Education **Association**, The Press **Club** of Dallas, the Headliners **Foundation**, and another one from the **Society** of Professional Journalists.

On their websites, many of these structures offer money whether labeled as a 'scholarship, award, reward, prize, contest, bursary'— you name it! So because scholarships are not always labeled as such, **make sure** that you are also broadening your keyword search with those listed above in quotation marks.

When looking for these structures, go to their websites at all levels relative to you. **For example:**

- National, state, regional, city, and chapter levels.

To quickly find a master list of such establishments, simply Google *your major* times the word 'professional organizations' and then from there find a website that has many listed.

Celebrity & Company Scholarships

Big companies also give out scholarships, such as — Google, Taco Bell, Amazon, Dr. Pepper etc. As mentioned earlier, I was recently able to help three students win such scholarships:

- Dr Pepper Tuition Giveaway ($100,000)
- Taco Bell Live Mas Scholarship ($5,000)
- Amazon Future Engineer Scholarship Program ($40,000)

However if you are to go for big and well-known scholarships, apply for those where the eligibility is less broad. Meaning, for example, you can only apply if:

- Your parent or you work for the company/part of the organization
- You are from a certain demographic (race, sexuality, etc.)
- You are from a certain region/state
- You are studying a specific major

In addition, some scholarships are in honor of specific people — like ones named after, famous athletes, artists, politicians etc. For example, the award from Jackie Robinson's Foundation.

I won two scholarships from living celebrities — one an artist, the other an athlete. And both were unrelated to my artistic or athletic history. Just make sure to keep tabs on influential people who you follow and their social media pages. If they're not giving out 'scholarships', they may be doing 'cash-giveaways' that they will personally send you via apps like CashApp, Paypal, Venmo, etc.

Click this link here for scholarships from famous people and companies that give scholarships: https://bit.ly/3o1GbsZ

Holiday & Holi-month Scholarships

There are quite a few scholarships specifically in honor of special holidays or months, such as Black History Month, Women's History Month, etc., — and a lot of times for these scholarships, you don't necessarily have to be part of that demographic to be awarded.

To easily find a calendar master list of special days, weeks, or months throughout the year, then please refer to these three links and then from there individually research and see if there are scholarships in honor of such days, weeks, or months:

- Month-long observances: https://bit.ly/3xObThw
- Holiday observances: https://bit.ly/2RvcJyZ
- Week-long observances:
  https://web-holidays.com/holiday-calendar/**may**-holidays
  -celebrations/may-week-long-observances/
  - (With this link, simply just **replace the month** seen in the URL by which month you are looking for)

However, note that sometimes with these scholarships they will require you to write (in addition to or by itself) an essay with a prompt that pertains to the holiday/month. The same can be said for scholarships that are named after historical/influential people. The application and its essay might ask something along the lines of, "How has this person impacted society/you?"

For these specific scholarships, you would have to do your research on what to say in your application so that you are catering to your audience. Personally, I've found that applying for scholarships based on personal essays rather than research or academic essays tends to be much easier to be awarded.

Scholarships For Minorities & White People

For people of color, and other minorities (such as relating to disability, sex/gender, sexuality etc.,) again, look into structures that are based around your demographic — or better yet overlap and intersect with various parts of your demographic/identity. For example, look up organizations such as:

- Foundations, associations, greek life, societies, funds, clubs etc.

And as for white students — the reality is that most scholarships are awarded to Caucasian-Americans according to the leading, U.S. national expert for financial aid, Mark Kantrowitz. I even personally interviewed him about this.

So, don't think or have this idea that only minority groups get scholarships. It's a myth. Look for scholarships where race isn't a factor. Focus on ones that are more so centered around merit, your major, community service, or your involvement in certain organizations.

Also on that note, a lot of times people think that scholarships that are funded by organizations geared towards certain demographics automatically mean that only people from that given background can apply. **However, this is not always true.**

I had a student — a white, non-Hispanic student — win a scholarship from the League of United Latin American Citizens (LULAC). Also, the student mentioned earlier who won the $100,000 scholarship from Dr. Pepper happened to win the same scholarship as me in 2020 from the AKA sorority. This sorority is for black women; however, he is Hispanic and male.

Alternative Ways To Find Scholarships

Important — Pay attention to emails or social media updates sent out from faculty, staff, and organizations you're involved in about scholarship and internship opportunities, especially if they are locally-based. You are more likely to get those!

I won six scholarships by simply doing this. Additionally, this advice has helped me secure multiple internships — three of which were all-expenses-paid — and one of which was from Disney/ABC News.

Also, if you are in a situation where your counselor or school isn't actively doing this, ask for them to start doing so! Or even personally seek someone else who can help you. When I was in high school, I had to use a counselor who wasn't even assigned to me because my main one was not helping at all.

Another tip is to keep tabs on local non-profits — whether they are well-established or fairly new. Especially ones that are centered around education and serving children/young adults.

Local nonprofits typically are the ones to give out scholarships, and if not that, other things you might need as a student. They may donate or give out things like:

- Clothes, laptops, free groceries, travel vouchers/grants, gift cards for living expenses, and so on.

So how exactly do you find nonprofits in your area? It's simple, really. Use this link here (https://www.guidestar.org/search) and from there type in your state. Once on there, make sure to not limit yourself to just the first tab of nonprofits that show up on the page — keep going!

Occasionally type in "scholarship" in a Google Search. From there, hit on the "news" tab and then press "search." You will see articles that were just written about new, ongoing, or recently awarded scholarships. You might get lucky and find one you can apply for!

Do the same by going to the "news" tab and specifically searching for your local news stations and papers while typing in the word "scholarship."

The first-ever scholarship I won was from simply watching the news!

Also on that note, Bold.org constantly uploads and creates scholarships every single month and lets students know via their email newsletter. I am in fact an ambassador for them and have a scholarship already running on their site, called "Pandemic's Box Scholarship" and plan on having even more sometime soon (after all part of the sales from this book goes towards creating scholarships that you can apply for).

- Link to my page: https://bold.org/donor/scholarshipguru/

Also, follow on social media (Facebook, Instagram, Twitter) news/entertainment, public figure accounts, and scholarship accounts. Here are some other scholarship accounts besides just mine to help you with your process: https://bit.ly/3xOlJA7

I've won two scholarships by occasionally doing this research technique. For instance, the scholarship I got from Future, the rapper. I saw on Instagram The Shade Room's post about it.

When searching, also type in the Google search engine keywords like 'award, reward, prize, grant, and contest' instead of just 'scholarship'.

Storytime: Receiving Scholarships I Was 'Ineligible For'

When I was in high school, I experienced three scholarship interviews:

- Two for black-male fraternities
- One by a Chinese-American foundation

Out of those three scholarships, I was awarded two of them:

- One from the black fraternity (despite being a woman).
- The other from the Chinese-American organization (despite being Black).

These scholarships had a **preference** for those who fit the target demographic. However, there was no rule saying that you have to be from that background. The application was **open to all.**

However, if it is clear that only those from a certain background are eligible, it's best not to be that person who doesn't qualify, yet still applies.

Or worse, that person who **fakes their identity** just to get a scholarship. **Please ... do not be that person.**

Also, there's the time I won a scholarship and free concert tickets from Future's foundation. Originally, I wasn't going to apply because it stated that you have to attend a school in one of the cities where the concert will take place during his tour. However, before submitting my application, I emailed his foundation asking if it was okay for me to still apply even though I go to school in North Texas and the concert was taking place all the way down in Austin which is in Central-Southern Texas. They said that it was fine, and I ended up winning the $2,000 scholarship the very next day. So, don't be afraid to apply for scholarships like this!

A similar story happened just recently. After having completed my undergraduate degree in broadcast journalism, I decided to go ahead and pursue graduate school (since I hope to one day become a journalism professor and you need your master's degree in order to be one). While scrolling through my emails sent out from my university, I came across one notifying students about a scholarship. The rules said that you had to be an undergraduate student. However, I emailed my professor and asked if I could apply as an incoming graduate student.

He said yes — and so I applied.

That scholarship ended up being worth $10,000 funded by NBC and also came with the benefits of internships and mentoring from NBC news professionals. My tuition is now fully paid for graduate school thanks to this scholarship.

So the moral of the story is — always ask, never assume that you are unqualified and can't apply!

Another thing I want to say about this is — **do not undermine and doubt yourself.** A lot of times people may say to me that simply because they don't have a high GPA or because they're not super involved in school, that they think there aren't any scholarships for them. Now, although those qualities do help with increasing your chances of winning, even if you do not have high stats, that shouldn't stop you from applying.

Instead, try to **find your domain and territory. It is still possible for you to win scholarships.** You just have to identify whatever redeeming/special quality about yourself that you can highlight in your application, which I will cover in part 3 of this book.

Community x Education Foundations

Just about every state in the U.S. (as well as some countries) has things called, "Community Foundations."

Even if you don't live in that particular region of the foundation's domain, as long as you live in the state, sometimes you are still eligible since you are a state resident or studying in the state. Also, if you are an out-of-state student, make sure to check out the foundations based within both the state you are originally from and where you will be studying.

Their scholarships — for whatever reason — sometimes never show up on general scholarship search engines like Fastweb or Unigo (might be because they were newly created). They are pretty hidden and have lots of private money — but thanks to that, that means that there are fewer people applying so you would have a better shot at winning — like I did TWICE (such as during my senior years of high school and college).

Use this link here and you will be redirected to an interactive map of all the community foundations based throughout the U.S. (there is also one in South Africa).

- https://www.cof.org/page/community-foundation-locator

When on the website, make sure to zoom in on the blue dots because some are so close together that there may just be several community foundations based around the same area.

After you have identified the foundations within your given state(s), create separate tabs for each one on your computer and individually research if they have scholarships that you are eligible for.

I happened to win two scholarships through these foundations during high school/college:

- The one from the Chinese-American organization
- Press Club of Dallas Scholarship

I say this so that you know that they typically have scholarships available for both high school students and ongoing/current college students.

And if you are in Texas like me, the site I used to win the two scholarships listed above was www.cftexas.org.

Once you get to one of these foundation's websites, simply do a quick CTRL-F or COMM-F on your computer to automatically find where on the page the "Scholarship" tab and portal are.

You will have to make a free account on their site. With that in mind, make sure to remember your username and password by noting them down somewhere secure!

There are also what is called, "Education Foundations" such as seen in Greek life and school districts. Sometimes you don't have to be a member to apply and win — such as the scholarships I won from a local **fraternity** my senior year of **high school**, and a **sorority** scholarship my senior year of **college!**

To quickly find a **master list of greek life organizations,** go to this site here: https://www.greekrank.com/ and create a separate tab for the sororities and the fraternities. Now, this will take some time — after all, there are hundreds of greek life organizations. So, I would recommend first starting with ones that you are more familiar with, then from there researching the others listed on the website. And once again, make sure to apply for not only their national awards but also state-level ones too.

International Student x Study Abroad

For me, studying abroad and receiving international student scholarships hasn't been my personal experience.

Originally, I was going to receive this experience by studying in Tokyo, Japan, and incorporating what I learned into this book. However, those plans were canceled due to COVID-19.

EVEN SO, I will try to do my best to help you.

If you are an international student, you can still apply the majority of the tips and advice seen in this book.

Here are several links to playlists I put together from various YouTubers who give scholarships and study abroad advice from all over the world!

- https://rb.gy/dvjogp

They range from US/Canada, Europe, Asia, Australia, Latin America, and Africa.

I will continue to add to this document as I gain more knowledge about scholarship advice as it pertains to certain countries and overall continents.

Also, here is another influencer who specializes in study abroad advice: www.tiktok.com/@packslight. Honestly, just check out her entire website because she is much more well-versed in knowing about study abroad opportunities than me and comes with experience! https://www.packslight.com/as-seen-on-tiktok

I will continue to add to the document listing study abroad influencers as I gain more knowledge about scholarship advice as it pertains to certain countries and overall continents.

www.youthop.com/scholarships/

Use the link above so that you can navigate scholarships and other opportunities by:

- Partial/fully funded
- Country/region
- Undergrad, grad, Ph.D.
- Exchange programs
- Grants/awards
- Internships/fellowships

Keep up with posts on the page linked below (and others like it by doing research) that posts about international scholarships!

- https://www.facebook.com/AScholarship/

Here are some more resources for finding international awards:

- https://express.adobe.com/page/Ebybi4QCyN5lc/
- https://scholarship-positions.com/
- www.fundingusstudy.org/StateSearch.asp
- www.iefa.org/
- https://foreign.fulbrightonline.org/apply
- www.scholars4dev.com/
- www.studyabroad.com/study-abroad-scholarships
- https://studentawards.com/scholarships/
- www.scholarshipscanada.com/ (for Canada)
- www.educanada.ca/scholarships-bourses/can/index.aspx (for Canada)

The scholarship process may be somewhat different for you because different countries have a variety of education systems with different demands. Or perhaps there exist stronger/weaker political and economic relations with other countries which may affect the availability of scholarships for you from certain places.

It's impossible for me to be the 'know-all expert' on every country's scholarship requirements and education systems — after all, there are nearly 200 countries.

However, despite not having the experience of being a student studying abroad or a student who is studying in a country outside of the U.S. — I have still helped so many people spanning from, **South Sudan, Ghana, D.R. Congo, Singapore, Indonesia, Canada, Germany**, and so on win scholarships.

With that being said, later on in Part 3 of this book, it will transition to constructing your scholarship essay which is the most important part of an application.

Also, if English is perhaps not your best-written language, I offer a service where I personally edit scholarship essays! To access this, you will have to sign into your Gmail account.

www.scholarship-guru.com/servicesproducts/essay-editing

Many have won as a result of this service, ranging from U.S. students to international students of various majors and study concentrations. By having the experience of winning mainly essay-based scholarships and being a journalism major who is currently working for Disney/ABC news at the national level — I am confident in my ability to edit and review essays. Also, my service can be used for internship and college admissions essays.

International Student Resources

NOTE: All of these links and the rest of the links in this book are directly listed on the **master-list URL** as seen towards the end of this book listed on the **services/products page**.

Additional resources for international scholarships:

Undergraduate and graduate scholarships and fellowships open to undocumented/DACA students:
https://spark.adobe.com/page/JjhGm5QwpCsto/

www.unigo.com/scholarships/by-type/international-student-scholarships

www.internationalstudent.com/scholarships/

www.edupass.org/paying-for-college/scholarships/databases/

www.affordablecolleges.com/resources/scholarships-for-international-students/

www.studyusa.com/en/a/536/scholarships-for-international-students-planning-to-study-in-the-usa

www.scholarships.com/financial-aid/college-scholarships/scholarships-by-type/international-student-study-abroad-scholarships/

https://www.iefa.org/scholarships

https://www.nafsa.org/about/about-international-education/financial-aid-study-abroad-undergraduate-students-resource

www.nafsa.org/about/about-international-education/students

Student Loan, Grants, & Trade School Scholarships

There are two main types of student loans — subsidized and unsubsidized. If you are offered loans for your education, the subsidized is better to accept. Why?

- **Subsidized** — Do not start adding interest to the loan until AFTER you leave college. These are only available to undergraduate students.
- **Unsubsidized** — Starts adding interest to the loan AS SOON AS the money is disbursed to your school. These are available to undergraduate and graduate students.

There are also: PLUS, Perkins, and bank loans for your education. Learn more about student loan types by going to this link here: www.t.ly/ncdM

If you have taken out loans or probably will eventually, there is a way for those loans to be 'forgiven' — in other words, you might only have to pay up to a certain amount, and the rest would be 'forgiven' over time by meeting certain criteria and obligations.

However, first thoroughly understand student loan forgiveness and some of the myths about it here: www.bit.ly/3kRK8yj. Also, make sure to **really watch over interest rates!** I've seen stories where others had to pay twice as much because of this. If you ever have to take out student loans, try your best to pay them off **as soon as possible!** The longer you wait, the more the interest rate will accumulate and add up over time.

So, if that means staying and living with your family as soon as your graduate, or rooming with others to cut back on living expenses — then so be it! If that means spending less money on shopping and take-out food — so be it! Go to the website shown below to learn all of what you need to know about properly coordinating and planning your finances as they relate to student loans: www.savingforcollege.com/student-loans

Refer to these two blogs here https://bit.ly/3b4FHwB and https://bit.ly/2RogpJf for **grants** that pay off student loans. There are grant programs for those going into the medical field, social work, law, research, veterinarian school, education/teaching etc., that pays part of if not all of your debt under certain conditions. Such as if you agree to teach in an underserved community for a certain amount of time.

- Scholarships **that pay loan debt**: https://bit.ly/3vKhRyh

- Scholarships for **vocational, technical, and trade school**: https://bit.ly/33gn5Wr

- Scholarships for **students returning to college/university**: https://bit.ly/33iFjqz

As far as federal grants, if you are a U.S. student, make sure that you fill out the FAFSA as soon as it opens every year on October 1st. Money is usually given out on a first-come, first-serve basis. **Apply here:** www.fafsa.gov + use **this checkoff list:** https://bit.ly/3oucczc **If you do not qualify for the FAFSA** as a U.S. student, or perhaps weren't awarded enough the last time around, then consider seeking other grant opportunities offered by states/territories: nasfaa.org/State_Financial_Aid_Programs

Also, look into **tuition reductions** here: https://bit.ly/3lc1UvB. And this free template provided by Going Merry on **appealing for more financial aid** from your school: https://bit.ly/3eV3FvF

Part 2

Optimization x Organization

Scholarship List and Templates

General Scholarship Info — The Folder

Before you fill an application out, have ready on hand this info listed in a **digital** online folder and a **physical** folder. This will save you a lot of time! Here's what the FOLDER should include (as PDFs):

- Your FAFSA — or the equivalent of this if you are an international student showing your financial aid
- Financial aid award letter for that school year
- Proof of enrollment (such as from the National Clearing House)
- Unofficial transcript + your official transcript (might have to pay your school like $10 to gain access to the official)
- Resume (modify as needed for scholarship)
- Cover letter (modify as needed for scholarship)
- Test score official papers (Example: SAT, ACT, GRE, AP)
- Letters of reference (have three minimum)
- Your digital signature (transparent .png file so to attach to your application/essay)
- Your professional headshot/a nice photo of yourself
- Picture file of official letterhead/logo from your;
  - university, those providing the scholarship, and those writing your reference letters
- Your EFC (Expected Family Contribution) from your FAFSA — or the equivalent for international students
- The dollar amount —
  - For a given semester or school year NOT cumulative over several years* listed individually that you have in (if so far) grants, scholarships, and loans

General Scholarship Info — The Document

- Your mailing address and your permanent address
  - (might differ — home vs. university)
- Your school's financial aid/scholarship mailing address, email, and phone number
- Contact info for letters of references
- Their emails + phone numbers
- Test scores — for example; SAT, ACT, GRE, etc.
- High school graduation date
- Your expected college graduation date
- Your cumulative GPA and/or major GPA
- Number of CUMULATIVE credit hours earned so far
- Number of MAJOR credit hours earned so far
  - If not sure of the number — contact your advisor!

Have you ever come across a job or internship application that required a lot of information, paperwork, and took hours to fill out, but because it was so time-consuming you ended up not applying? Well, the same can be said with scholarship applications.

I can't tell you how many scholarships and internships I have applied for where I felt like just quitting right in the middle because the application seemed as if it were endless. However, had I given up on such applications that required more work I wouldn't have been awarded the scholarship from the **U.S. Congress** or my internship with **Disney/ABC News.**

That's why I want you to get organized so that you do not feel exhausted by the process and end up missing deadlines or giving up altogether. You may be *this close* to preventing yourself from a breakout opportunity that shapes your future.

Usernames & Passwords

We've all been there. We forget our usernames and passwords to our emails and the services we signed up for. And more than likely, that will continue to happen to you throughout this whole, entire, tedious scholarship process. That's why you should have saved somewhere all your usernames and passwords for things relating to scholarships and your overall education.

Preferably, have your passwords/usernames saved somewhere physical that you can remember, and you know you won't lose. But if you are forgetful about keeping track of physical things, it might be best for you to instead have that information digital — whether that's on your online drive, a physical flash drive, or in the private, code/pin protected note section on your devices.

To make it easier on yourself, have all your passwords and usernames the same or similar to the ones you already use.

And as far as **more sensitive information** — such as your social security number, and access to your bank account — try to have that information memorized in your head!

From my years of experience with applying for scholarships, here's a list of the things you should have saved securely somewhere. **Username/password for:**

- Financial aid website (FAFSA)
- Student loan website
- Scholarship search engine websites or apps
  - (Example: Unigo, Fastweb etc.)
- Scholarship application portals
- School admissions portals

- The answers to your security questions
- Access to test scores online
    - (Example: SAT, ACT, AP, GRE testing etc.)
- Routing number + banking number (some awards might send the scholarship to you this way)
- Social security number
    - This is required when applying for financial aid through grants and loans (Example: FAFSA)

As mentioned earlier, typically, a scholarship should not ask for your social security number. However, some legit scholarships may only ask for the last four digits of your social security or perhaps the full number. If you happen to have a scholarship like this, double and triple-check the legitimacy of the scholarship!

Create An Online Scholarship List

MENTION:

- Name of scholarship
- Copy and paste URL of scholarship (if it has one)
- Due Date + time + time zone
- Date of when results will be out
  - If stated — if not stated, ask around when results will be out!
- Organize scholarships by due date/month and type
  - Example: major-based, university-given etc.
- Note if it requires electronic recommendation letters
  - Meaning, those that the person writing your recommendation has to go to an online portal themselves, rather than you submitting their written letter via an attached PDF document.
  - If so, take note of that so to give those people more time so to meet the deadline!
- Amount of Scholarship
  - Indicate if it's refundable, renewable, four-year, two-year, one-time, can reapply etc.
- Note if it has to be mailed in and/or postmarked by a certain date
  - That way you can have more time preparing instead of doing it last minute
- Indicate and highlight when you have COMPLETED and SUBMITTED the application.
- If you submitted the application but are still waiting on electronic reference letters to come in, consider writing 'pending' next to that scholarship listed as a reminder to yourself that you still need that paperwork.

Also, take the time to contact again those you chose to do the recommendation letters so to remind them to get it done in time! The last thing you want is to miss a deadline!

It might actually help you to tell those people a **fake deadline** of when you need it by, that way you can minimize having to stress about whether or not they will meet the actual deadline in time.

And lastly, your online scholarship list doesn't necessarily have to be very optimized. As long as it is functional for you and you are staying on top of deadlines — that's all that really matters.

It also helps to take note of these deadlines on a **digital calendar** as opposed to a physical one because you can receive alerts as reminders of when it is due.

Also, check out on my website some blogs I put together of scholarships based on study concentration, grade level, race, gender, and so on.

Scholarship mini-database: https://bit.ly/scholarshipguru

Please note that this is a mini-database of scholarships and some of the blogs are continuing to be updated periodically. I would recommend that you mainly focus on more in-depth databases out there for scholarships.

Also, please **download** and refer to this very comprehensive **College 101 Field Guide** (https://bit.ly/3xLZlY6). This is especially helpful for those trying to get college admissions scholarships for their undergraduate or graduate degree. This free guide was put together by Nelia Ekeji, a college advisor. It provides you with so much information such as: a senior year timeline, steps to applying for college, free study guides for ACT / SAT and so much more!

Organizing Scholarship Essays

When making your scholarship list, indicate the type of essay needed and the word count minimum.

Preferably, apply for scholarships based on personal essays about your life, academic, and career goals.

However, you might also apply for ones that are research-based or have a prompt that pertains outside of your personal life.

If applying for these types, note this on your list of scholarships. Why? Because these will more than likely take you much longer to write since you are not writing about yourself, but something that you have to do research about. Meaning — these are the types of essays that you really should not be writing last minute!

Also, to stay on top of deadlines, it helps me to title the file name of essays as something like:

DueDate_NameOfScholarship_MyName

Then when you are done with writing your essay, simply delete the "DueDate" part of the file name and export the document as a PDF file to submit your scholarship application.

Another thing I want to note about your scholarship essays or even recommendation letters — especially those that you reuse for other applications — is to make sure you reread over them to ensure that what is written is up-to-date. See, I accidentally submitted my reused essays and letters for other applications and later noticed that the writing was either outdated (as in it was in the tense from when I was in a different school year) or even it was written out to a different audience.

My Personal Scholarship List + Template

My personal scholarship list example: https://bit.ly/312UzXJ

This should give you an idea of what your scholarship list should look like as outlined previously in the book. You might even find on my list some scholarships listed that you are eligible for — who knows!

Also, your list doesn't have to be highly optimized — just as long as it is functional for you and you are staying on top of deadlines!

Google doc template linked here: https://bit.ly/3kV7O4D

Google spreadsheet template linked here: https://bit.ly/2EcYfgy

Also, here are all 30+ of the scholarships I have ever won:

https://bit.ly/2PZDesn

I also want to encourage you to put these scholarship deadlines on your calendar as well. With me, I create lots of documents and so by only having these scholarships mentioned on your list, you are very prone to missing the deadlines. So, make sure to also have it mentioned on your calendar. Preferably your digital calendar on your phone because we carry our phones just about everywhere.

Another tip is to **apply for scholarships in bulk** rather than spacing it out over time. This can especially be helpful if closer to the actual deadline you are suddenly overwhelmed by work, life, school, or even your physical/mental health. At least then you won't have to worry about missing scholarship deadlines.

Using Google Applications

Google Drive and Google Docs will be your best friends during this whole, tedious, scholarship process. It's best to use some type of online drive instead of a physical flash drive or just your computer's hard drive because when it's online — you can apply from any computer with Wi-Fi.

Create hyperlinks over the name of the scholarship leading directly to webpages for scholarships you are trying to apply for. To do so, follow these steps:

- Copy the URL of the scholarship site
- Highlight the name of the scholarship in your list / spreadsheet document
- Hold, CTRL - K (for PCs) or COMM - K (for MACs)
- Paste in the URL in and press "apply" or "enter/return" on your keyboard — and that's it!

When on a Google Doc, you can also 'write' your essay by using voice-typing. I did this for the essay/scholarship I won from Future! To access this, press on your keyboard:

- MAC: COMM-SHIFT-S
- PC: CTRL-SHIFT-S

Google's voice function is fairly accurate (much more accurate than Apple's Siri from my personal experience) and if you want to learn how to use it and all of the voice commands it can do, click this link here: https://bit.ly/3kTjoPr.

You can do the same with Microsoft Word using the "dictate" function.

Note that according to Google:

- Voice commands are available only in English. The account language and document language must both be English.
- Voice commands are not available in [Google] Slides speaker notes. (However, voice-typing is still functional).

Examples of some of the voice commands you can use include:

- **Text formatting:** bold, italicize, underline, capitalize, etc.
- **Editing document:** copy, paste, cut, insert link, etc.
- **Editing tables:** insert table, insert row, insert column etc.
- **Select text:** select all, select word, select match text etc.
- Resume and stop voice-typing

I would highly recommend using this function especially if you are better at articulating your thoughts via speaking aloud rather than typing/writing this out.

Also, if you want to multitask like I did (I spoke out my essay while eating a late-night snack), then this would be great for that as well!

Refer to this blog here https://bit.ly/3emW3TC for free Google add-ons that you can use that not only can help you with strengthening the quality of your writing, but also any aspect of education — even for a math class.

Time Zones

When making your list of scholarships you want to apply for, take note of the time zone.

Let's say that a scholarship based in **New York** is due **11:59 p.m.** Eastern Time (EST):

- **Texas** uses Central Standard Time (CST or CT), therefore one hour behind New York.
    - So, in Texas, that means the scholarship is due one hour before @ **10:59 p.m. CT.**
- **California** uses Pacific Standard Time (PST), therefore three hours behind New York.
    - In California, that same scholarship is due three hours before @ **8:59 p.m. PST.**

Google and convert the time zone. Or you can go to this site to find out this information: www.thetimezoneconverter.com/

Don't be like me where I thought I was on time for a certain scholarship but ended up not being and wasted my time!

If the time zone isn't indicated on the scholarship, email or call those over the scholarship, and ask them! Sometimes you can guess this based on the listed physical address of the scholarship on their website.

International/study abroad students should especially watch out for time zones. Again, this is where it comes in handy to write down on your calendar the deadlines for not just scholarships but anything that you have to do that has a deadline.

Organize Physical Scholarship Applications

You might be doing your scholarship search one day and come across one that is due that exact same day or the next day!

You might even be in a situation where you don't have access to a printer/internet — or perhaps the printer/internet decides to stop working right then and there (happened to me so many times).

So, here's a list of things that you should have already printed out and supplied — organized in a folder or binder — to save yourself a lot of time.

- Large envelopes + stamps
- Resume + cover letter
- Essays (250, 500, 1,000-word versions)
- Letters of recommendation
- Test score official papers
- Financial aid paperwork
  - FAFSA, previous financial aid package award letters year-by-year, and scholarship award letters
- Unofficial + official transcripts
  - May have to be enclosed in an envelope with an official seal by your school

Also when mailing off your application, I would encourage you to get a tracking number for your package and track it periodically online. I have had cases where my application was **lost in the mail** or accidentally put in the wrong postal box. So, after a couple of days have passed since you mailed it off, email or call those over the scholarship to confirm if your application has been received.

Don't Miss Deadlines

Check your scholarship listing document/spreadsheet often. Write down on your digital calendar when scholarships are due and set alerts on the calendar indicating the exact time it is due.

Better yet — **trick yourself** by stating on your calendar and scholarship list that the scholarship is due one or two hours or better yet days before when it is actually due.

Since I am a major procrastinator, I do this to help prevent myself from applying too late — this is especially the case for scholarships that require more attention. For instance, those that:

- Require electronic reference letters
  - Of where the people writing your letters of recommendation have to go into the scholarship portal themselves to submit it rather than you submitting it yourself as a PDF attachment.
- Require to be postmarked by a certain date

Also, about postmarking — many post offices close on Sundays. So, if the scholarship needs to be postmarked by Sunday at the latest — or perhaps there's a holiday that will close offices — that means you need to get your application sent in before!

For one scholarship I won, it happened to be due on Indigenous People's Day (October 12, 2019). So, offices were closed, but that was the last day I could submit my application. I had to negotiate for my application to be submitted the day after.

When You Have Too Much Scholarship Money

Some schools have things called "scholarship displacement," or aka, "stacking." This refers to when any need-based financial aid your school awarded you (like grants, loans, and work-study) is reduced after you win a private scholarship.

Typically, they might reduce the same amount of money you got from the scholarship(s) by reducing or completely taking away your loan (which might be okay for you since loans you have to pay them back).

However, you don't want them to reduce or completely take away your work-study or grant(s).

This happened to me during my freshman year of college. I won a scholarship, but my expenses for that year were basically already covered. So, instead of them rolling it over into the next school year when I would actually need the scholarship, the Financial Aid Department simply took away my grant money and replaced it with the scholarship money.

So essentially, they **took away free money and replaced it with free money.** Meaning there was no point in even winning the scholarship in the first place.

Also on that note, let's say that you are one of the most qualified applicants for several university-funded scholarships that you applied for. Even though you are one of the top choices, most of the time they can only award you one or two of those awards because they don't want to 'over-award' a student, but instead share the wealth with other students. That is why you cannot be dependent on solely applying to college-funded scholarships.

Preventing Scholarship Displacement

To prevent your grant or scholarship money from being reduced or completely taken away — communicate with your school's financial aid department/office. Ask them if they can **replace/reduce** the money offered to you through loans or student employment (work-study). That way, you can use the scholarship money and grant money awarded to you.

Like me, you may be in a situation where if your scholarship is used this semester/year, it will reduce or take away other financial aid. If this is the case, ask the main point of contact for your scholarship if you can **defer your scholarship** for future use. Financial aid awarded to you may be more or less as you progress through your years at school, so this might be a better option.

For instance, had I known in advance that my father would get a raise from his job — which would in turn make me ineligible for the Pell Grant my junior year of college — I would have deferred some of the scholarship money awarded to me from my second year of college to my third year instead.

Another way is to consider **increasing your cost of attendance** for that given semester/school year. Doing this will allow you to keep more of the scholarship money, which you can then use for other essentials you might need for your education (like a new laptop, educational software etc). Locate online or ask your college for a **"cost of attendance adjustment form."**

And lastly, research the **financial aid policy** of your school as well as the grant policy from wherever you got your grant from. For instance, I got a Texas grant, so I would read that fine print.

It's already hard enough as is to get a scholarship. Just imagine if your existing financial aid, such as grants were taken away from you because you were awarded a scholarship, and then you are forced to take out a student loan.

So again, look up the policies for financial aid from your university. Research the financial aid policy if you were awarded a grant — such as from your state, a private company, or a national one like the Pell Grant. If you don't understand what the terms and conditions of the grant are saying, then get a professional to look at it, such as someone who is well-versed in financial aid policy.

I would highly recommend that you take the time to look into the site linked below to help navigate through this process and read their various articles on how to save for college / university: https://www.savingforcollege.com/

Also on that note, make sure to take into consideration what type of scholarship it is that you are awarded. Some scholarships are tuition only, or perhaps only for external expenses — such as for housing, transportation, meal plan etc,. Sometimes the type of award is explicitly outlined in the terms and conditions section of the application, and other times you will have to contact that scholarship committee to learn what type it is.

So, if you have already been awarded a full-tuition scholarship from your university and then you are awarded an external scholarship that can only be applied to tuition — unfortunately in that case you will have to forfeit one of those scholarships. This is when you would weigh which scholarship holds more value. By this I mean sometimes a scholarship is only a scholarship, whereas others might come with other benefits such as internships, mentoring, and an active community.

Using A Scholarship To Pay Student Loans

It is possible to be awarded many scholarships but still graduate with student loan debt as seen in this article from U.S. News: https://bit.ly/2F4yghF. This can be a result of what was covered in the previous chapter about "scholarship displacement."

In most cases, scholarships will make the money out to your school and from there will adjust your financial aid package. **However** — some external scholarships might write the check in your name, and indicate that you can use it however you want.

If you have a scholarship like this, and you happen to have student loans that still need to be paid off, this might be a great way of doing that. Or perhaps if you have other things you want — like a new laptop for school — you can use this money.

If the external scholarship given to you says that they make the checks out to your school, try to negotiate for them to make the check to you. Strategically communicate to them (preferably via email) your situation and how if the check is made out to your school, they will reduce or take away your existing financial aid, whereas if it is made out to you, it will be put to good educational use.

You can also use scholarships to pay off student loans with the excess that is refunded back to you from your university. If you have financial aid that exceeds tuition for that given semester, you will get a refund check in either one or several installments sometime towards the beginning of the semester. Here is a list of some scholarships that pay off student loan debt. Some students I recommended these opportunities to were able to win and have their debt wiped out: https://bit.ly/debtscholarships

Getting Paid To Go To School With Scholarships

According to the leading, national researcher for financial aid, Mark Kantrowitz, "Of students in Bachelor's degree programs in 2015-16, only 1.5 percent got enough scholarships and grants to cover 100 percent of the cost of attendance."

This percentage is even smaller for those who happen to get so much funding that it exceeds the money needed to attend school.

In very rare cases — some winning students have gotten paid to go to school.

This could be you too.

Read these two articles on how these two students were able to get paid anywhere from $3,000 to $4,000 per school year in excess scholarship money:

- "I graduated with thousands of dollars left over" https://cnn.it/31Zlkfc
- "What happens if you win more scholarships than you need?" https://bit.ly/2YcnGWK

Multiply Your Awarded Scholarship Money

There are quite a few scholarships out there that are renewable as long as you meet certain conditions (such as by maintaining your GPA, community service hours etc.,) or that you can apply for again even if you were already awarded in the past.

So many times, students forget to take note of the scholarships they've received that have conditions like this and forget to reapply or request a renewable one.

To stay on top of this, have those scholarships listed in a separate document, with the needed contact info and deadlines indicated.

Keep in touch with the scholarship committee — update them on what you have achieved throughout the semester/school year.

Write a thoughtful thank you note on how the scholarship has helped you so far ever since you were awarded it months or even years ago. Sometimes scholarships may instead require you to provide a thank you video, so be prepared for that as well!

The more of a personal connection you have with them, and the more appreciative you are, the more likely they are to award you more money.

Also, sometimes scholarships you have won in the past cannot be reapplied to for your undergraduate degree, but instead, you can reapply for it when you pursue a different degree, such as for getting your master's in graduate school. In that case, make sure to also take note of that.

Part 3

Constructing Your Essay

Winning Excerpts and What To Write

The Heart of Your Scholarship Application

The vast majority of scholarship applications require some sort of essay or short answer section — some may even require both.

A strong essay is essential if you want to win. You are up against some people with not only strong academic and leadership backgrounds but also strong writing skills. If you fall short of that, you might not be awarded.

As mentioned earlier in the previous part of this book, **the essay** is what allows your application to go from being just a number out of hundreds to thousands of other applicants to be seen as an individual with your own story and experiences.

It humanizes your application.

To make sure that your paper is grammatically correct, use www.grammarly.com/ or Microsoft's Editor add-on. Both offer free versions.

If you want me to edit your essay, I also offer a service for that linked here: https://bit.ly/2FMfBCt. I understand that not everyone has the same level of literacy or writing skills whether that's due to educational barriers or English not being someone's first or best language. Even so, I believe that access to funding for higher education shouldn't be denied based on this.

Refer To Previous Winners Essay(s)

If you have access to old essays from those who previously won the scholarship you want — then read and study them.

Or perhaps if it's not available online, you might know someone personally who won the scholarship in the past. In that case, reach out to them and ask if they could send you their essay so you can have an idea for — not to copy — but as a reference on what the scholarship committee is looking for as far as:

- Content, format, and writing style

Study and take note of how they:

- Start off their essay and how the conclude their essay.
- Transition from paragraph to paragraph covering different elements/ideas.
- How they use their language.
  - Does the language come across as conversational? Professional? Perhaps a mixture of both?
  - Do they incorporate figurative language such as:
    - Anaphoras
    - Personification
    - Metaphors
    - Similes
    - Symbolisms
    - Hyperboles
  - What about imagery, alliteration, etc?

Now, if you don't have previous winning essays to read as an option, the next page will explain how to format your personal scholarship essay.

48

Scholarship Essay Formula

Trials to triumphs — your humble beginnings

- A 'trial' can be something like your family's financial difficulties growing up, or even how you struggled in a class. It doesn't necessarily have to be something traumatic or involve very sensitive information.
- Also, do not sound self-pitying! Be humble. At some point after reading so many hard-life essays, the person evaluating might get desensitized to those types.
- After mentioning your life's trial, you will transition to how you perhaps grew from that and/or overcame it despite your situation. And if you haven't quite yet overcome that yet, mention how you are trying to by pursuing an education.

Major & Career Goals

- If your 'trials to triumphs' happen to be what inspired you to pursue a certain major, this could be where you would say that as a new paragraph.
- Talk about what you have accomplished so far with your studies and/or what you hope to accomplish once you start your studies/career.

Family / Financial statement

- Such as illness, disability, divorce, death, etc.

Your work so far pertaining to your career goals

- Such as related classes/courses, extracurricular activities, organizations, clubs, and community service

How receiving the scholarship will help you

- Sound as humble as possible and mention the name of the scholarship in this part of your essay so that it feels custom-made for those evaluating your scholarship essay!

If not too restrained by the word count, then also include:

- Life goals (if possible, make it tie into your studies)
- Community involvement related to your goals
- Leadership Position(s)
- Reason for going to college, and/or that specific college
- Role models who motivated you

NOTE: Use famous quotes sparingly. Oftentimes, it might just be better to not use them at all. Also, typically do not start off your essay with a famous quote (like from a celebrity, philosopher, or scripture). If you do use one, incorporate it in the middle, or towards the end of your essay.

Another tip is to try not to use overly fancy vocabulary in your essays. If you are trying to use a word that the average person wouldn't use in conversational speaking or even know exists, then it's probably best not to use it. The last thing you want is for someone to have to look up in a dictionary to understand what you are even talking about. Also by doing so it may give off the impression that you are trying too hard to impress them and sound 'intelligent'.

Speak from the heart. That will have much of a greater impact on your reader rather than trying to sound like a philosopher.

My Scholarship Essay | 'Trials To Triumphs' Excerpt

About the scholarship:

❖ 2020-2021 Edward O. Fritts Scholarship, sponsored by the Broadcast Education Association (BEA)
❖ Nationally competitive for media concentrations

The essay starts off showing my original career goals, then goes into how and why that changed.

- **Trials**: The second paragraph highlights my strong work ethic and how I nearly dropped out of my class.
- **Triumphs**: The hard work paid off and I ended up excelling and exceeding expectations.

"Originally, I got into journalism because I thought I wanted to be a news reporter and anchor. However, now, I have an aspiration to be a news/show producer.

I realized this after finishing an 8-hour class where everyone else was upperclassmen — such as seniors and graduate students — I was only a sophomore at the time. The class was meant to replicate an actual newsroom on a 9 - 5 workday. We were expected to stack the show, come up with story ideas for general news, entertainment, and sports, film, and edit videos as well as write and edit scripts, and later it aired on our school's cable channel. The class was highly demanding and stressful, and I felt unqualified in the beginning, nearly dropping out of the class. My professor said at the beginning that typically only one or two students get an "A" in her class and those who do are more than ready and qualified to work in actual newsrooms.

Needless to say, after putting in 10x the amount of work than others and exceeding the expectations of both my professor and classmates, I ended up receiving the highest grade in the class."

A final note:

As you can see from this excerpt from my essay I didn't talk about a traumatic experience in my life. Oftentimes when I read other people's essays they talk about things that are very sensitive to them — things which they perhaps haven't even shared with people they know personally.

So, why should you share something that is so sensitive that you haven't even shared with those in your personal life?

Don't sell your soul for scholarship money, or even for a school admissions essay (both of which are essentially the same). If you don't feel comfortable sharing that side of yourself — then don't.

Also, think of it this way — since many people have this misconception that the only way to write scholarship or college admissions essays is to talk about **trauma,** over time those evaluating the applications may get **desensitized** to constantly seeing essay after essay formatted the same.

Just as how many people tend to avoid watching the news because after some point in time it becomes too depressing to watch — that same burnout can happen if someone is overly exposed to too many sad stories.

My Scholarship Essay | 'Conclusion' Excerpt

About the scholarship:

- ❖ Advancement of Women in Sports and Entertainment scholarship, funded by Floyd Mayweather's Foundation
- ❖ Nationally competitive for undergraduate women in media concentrations (2019 winner)
- In the conclusion, this is where you insert the name of the scholarship so that it sounds more personalized (addressing your audience) to the scholarship committee reading it.
- Try to use in your essay "to further my academic/career endeavors" when answering how the scholarship will help you.

"If awarded the Advancement of Women in Sports and Media scholarship through the Floyd Mayweather foundation, it would greatly help assist me in further pursuing my academic and career endeavors with a bit less of a concern on financing my education. The less I have to worry about money, the more time I have on my hands to dedicate to learning, creating, and seeking out experiences to polish my skills and set myself up for success."

My Scholarship Essay | 'Sound Humble' Excerpt

About the scholarship:

- ❖ I Am A Dreamer scholarship from Future's Freewishes Foundation (2019 winner)
- Avoid saying, "I deserve," or even, "I should be awarded"
- Don't sound like "pick me!"
- Be indirect in how you approach it.
- In this essay I didn't, but in the previous excerpt, I tend to start with, "If awarded ***insert scholarship name*** ..."

"If awarded **this** scholarship, it would greatly help assist my academic endeavors because like I mentioned earlier, I am constantly applying and searching for scholarships (dedicating up to 2-3 hours per day) but keep getting denied time, after time, after time again because as a current college student, I'm dealing with a pool of less than 10 percent of scholarships I can apply for. It can be discouraging, but in a way, it is humbling to be denied. It reminds me that I am not entitled to any scholarship and that the other person who won it is just as deserving. It's not my place to envy their blessing when my own blessing may just be in the final stages of shipping its way into my life."

This is one example of how to sound humble in your writing. It is important to do so because oftentimes when I edit essays they may come across as entitled to win or as if they are begging. You don't want to give them that impression. If you have ever watched the film Charlie and the Chocolate Factory, throughout the film Charlie was humble from the very beginning — unlike the other children — and thanks to his character he won the competition despite not being as accomplished as the other kids.

My Scholarship Essay | 'Thank You' Excerpt

Again, here is another example from the scholarship I won from Future, the rapper. This scholarship was basically a hybrid between nationally, state-wide, and locally competitive. It all depended on where he was touring in the U.S. for that specific night.

Some things to consider mentioning in this portion of your essay include to:

- Write a brief thank you to those reading your essay in one to two sentences.
- Mention how exactly you would use this scholarship.
- Mention that you would like to create your own scholarship one day.

"With that being said, I just want to thank Future and everyone behind the *I'm A Dreamer* scholarship fund. A $2,000 scholarship may seem like nothing to some, but for me, that would fund an entire class including a meal plan going into the spring semester. I aspire to create my own scholarship fund one day, so to see that this opportunity is made available to current college students – I would love for there to be more like this moving forward."

The Thank You Note

Can state your "thank you" in:

- Your essay
- An email
- Or if the application has a section that asks, "Is there anything else you want to add for consideration in the scholarship selection process?" — then add it there.
- You can state the thank you note multiple times such as via email and in your essay!

It can say something along the lines of:

- "Thank you for making this scholarship available to students. Anyways, whoever is reading this, I hope you have a great/blessed day!"

This technique also works for job and internship applications.

I have found that it is much more effective saying a thank you note during the application process rather than after the fact when you have already been awarded. It shows that you are appreciative of what they are doing whether or not you are even awarded. Therefore, that may incline them to award you over someone else because you seem very humble and modest.

However, don't overdo it! You don't want to make it too obvious that you are trying to kiss up to them. Be professional and subtle in going about it. You perhaps could even mention why you appreciate even more what they are doing. Such as mentioning the importance this holds for first-generation students, minorities, those in your given major, and so on.

Saying This Will Almost Guarantee That You Win

Mention that you want to create a scholarship fund in the future. Scholarship committees love to hear that because it shows that you are like-minded to them.

If not that, something like creating a charity or non-profit.

This ties back into 'relatability' and 'knowing your audience'.

I did this technique for the three scholarships that I won Fall of 2019 that were shown previously as excerpts:

- One from Floyd Mayweather $1,000 (the boxer)
- One from Future $2,000 (the rapper)
- And the BEA broadcasting scholarship $1,000

If you want to take it a step further, elaborate on what type of scholarship you are looking to create.

Such as if you want there to be more financial opportunities for students from your specific demographic and/or study concentration. Consider elaborating on how investing in this particular niche will have a positive impact on the future, whether that's locally, nationally, or globally.

Another tip is to mention somewhere in your essay how if selected for the scholarship it would be an investment in not only you but others as well — such as in your family or even if you are going into a career that is about helping others. The scholarship committee may feel more compelled to award you because they would feel that their money is being put to even further good use by someone who will pay it forward.

The Magic Touch Of Stand-Alone Sentences

One-sentence paragraphs should be used for dramatic effect.

They add a lot of character to your essay, leaving a strong impression on those reading it.

These should be used sparingly — I typically will use anywhere from one to three in my essays.

Overusing them will make your essay choppy.

To incorporate these into your essay, use when:

There is a transition between two opposing moods/tones —

"Despite the challenges I faced, I wasn't going to let that define or deter me from my aspirations."

Incorporate when there's a moment of self-realization —

"Through that experience, from there on out — I knew what my calling was in life."

When you state your personal beliefs/philosophy —

Example from my essay: "One's literacy level should not dictate or define one's intelligence level."

Stand-alone sentences can easily become the most memorable sentence throughout your entire essay, so make every word count! Think of it as a news article headline. You want your writing to be remembered even when the committee reviews hundreds or thousands of applicants after looking over yours.

Addressing the Prompt - Do's and Don'ts

Let's say that the prompt for the scholarship essay is "What is your primary goal for going to school?"

Don't directly address the prompt within the first sentence by just reiterating what was already asked, for instance, saying, "My primary goal for going to school is to ..."

Doing that is basic and is amateur writing. Your essay simply won't stand out.

Also, don't say, "I deserve this scholarship because ..." Once again, that's immature writing!

Instead, use the steps as indicated earlier in this part of the book covering the 'scholarship essay formula'.

A good place to start your essay with is a "flashback" where you show "personal growth" after overcoming a challenge (ex. of "trials to triumph") that ended up being a defining moment for yourself — especially if you can link it to your future aspirations.

Also, don't use language that comes across as if you're begging to be awarded or insinuating that you are better than other applicants just because of your accomplishments. Be humble!

If you are still struggling with how to sound humble and inspirational with your writing, I would highly suggest that you watch TedTalks and NPR's Story Corps series. Links here:

- https://www.ted.com/talks
- https://www.npr.org/series/4516989/storycorps

Know Your Audience

If the scholarship that you are wanting to apply for is through an organization, company, foundation, club, society etc., — know your audience, and what their values are.

You can identify this information by going to their mission statement as seen on their social media or website. It might help your application process if you mention those keywords so that they better identify with your essay.

However, **don't overuse** those words to the point where it is obvious that you are trying to kiss up to them! It might be better to **use synonyms** for those words so that what you're doing isn't as obvious!

If you happen to personally know those behind the scholarship and their values, mention something that you think they can really relate to.

If you happen to be applying for a scholarship and they don't have a website, there are other ways to go about this such as:

- If the scholarship is named after someone, look into the background of that person and their personal values.
- Draw conclusions based on appearance.

Another thing to note regarding knowing your audience is to omit certain things from your writing or even what you say during a scholarship interview depending on what you have interpreted to be the values of the selection committee. For instance, older generation people probably won't understand or care for certain topics, unfortunately.

The Most Common Question Sections

Some scholarships don't necessarily ask for an "essay" but instead — or in addition — "short answers." Your response to each will either be limited by word or character count:

- State your career goals
- State your High School and list the honors, activities, membership/leadership roles held
- State your College and list the honors, activities, membership/leadership roles held
- Professional and/or College experience
  - (as it relates to your field of study)
- Relevant coursework
  - (as it relates to your field of study)
- Describe other accomplishments
  - (outside of school — community-related)
- Describe other experiences
  - (outside of work and school)
- Describe other employment
  - (position(s) held + duties/responsibilities + what you learned)
- Community Service
  - (position(s) held + duties/responsibilities + what you learned and how you grew)
- What else should the scholarship committee know when considering you for this award?
- Are there any other outside financial circumstances not already addressed in your FAFSA?
- How much funding do you have so far?
  - (student loans, grants, outside scholarships, family contribution, pay from job(s), etc.)

Now that that has been established, I want you to take the time and look over the questions listed below. Write down a general outline of how you would answer each one. When addressing these questions, try to aim towards answering them by incorporating some of if not all of the following:

- **Who** – who did you affect and who did you work with?
- **What** – what did you do and what did you learn?
- **When** – when did this happen and for how long?
- **Where** – where were you physically and where were you mentally before that experience vs. after that experience?
- **Why** – why did you do that and why is it important?
- **How** – how did you do that and how did you impact others? How did others impact you?

Answering these questions will help with making your writing much more holistic and impactful for those reading your essay. It will also ensure that there are no gaps in the story you are conveying. You can answer these questions as they relate to:

- Your studies
- Internships
- Research
- Towards your career
- Community service
- Familial relations
- Friendships
- Mentorships

How You Should Answer These Sections

NOTE: When answering, generally, use complete sentences so you can elaborate!

If stating your membership in an organization, don't just end at naming the organization and what your title/position is — expand because that organization's name and what it does might not be self-explanatory or well-known. For instance —

- **Non-self-explanatory:** "I am a member of NABJ."
- **Explanatory:** "I am an active member of the National Association of Black Journalists (NABJ), the largest organization for journalists of color in the United States.

NOTE: Depending on who your audience is for an application, a non-self-explanatory element might actually be explanatory. For instance, if I am applying for a journalism scholarship, they will more than likely know what NABJ is. Whereas if I were to apply for a non-journalism award, they might not know.

Briefly summarize in one to three sentences your duties and what the organization is all about. And if possible, tie in elements of this to the values and mission statement the scholarship foundation has.

This is also a great place to insert a moment of reflection on how being a part of that organization, event, initiative, etc,. helped you grow as a person — such as certain skills and life lessons you acquired.

If it is more so community service-based, then you would instead want to mainly highlight how you impacted others.

How I Answered These Question Sections

Sometimes it might be better to just answer these question sections as bullet points — such as your awards, honors, and extracurriculars.

This is especially the case for applications with character word limits where you have less writing space allowed.

Here's how I answered some of these questions on two winning scholarships using two methods:

Answering with complete sentences: https://adobe.ly/3iKmFwU

Answering as listed points: https://adobe.ly/36xA3zD

Also, again, consider your audience! There may be certain things that you traditionally would not mention on your application but decide to say specifically for a certain application because you assume those evaluating it will resonate with it more.

And also, on that note, if there is something that you usually include but don't feel would be appropriate for a particular application — then feel free to omit that for now.

If within your response you would like to mention a certain URL link, make sure that you use a link shortener website (whether or not you have character or word count limits). Long URLs will distract the reader from your writing, and simply just look tacky. So, if you have the opportunity to paste it in — or better yet hyperlink to it — feel free to do so.

Formatting Your Essay

- Justified format
- Size 12 font
- Use page numbers (bottom left corner)
- For font use: Calibri, Arial, Times New Roman
  - Some scholarships require Times New Roman
- Use — hyphens — in your writing. I do this a lot.
  - It adds character and emphasis to my essay to really draw out certain points.
- Use 1.5 line spacing
  - Unless mandatory to have double-spaced

Why I tend not to double-space essays (unless required):

- It makes the essay look longer to read and adds pages.
- You don't want the person reading to feel overwhelmed because they've probably already read hundreds of essays that sound the same and look the same or appear long.

Make sure that your paragraphs aren't too bulky! It creates the illusion that the paper is too congested. Space it out with three to six sentence paragraphs. If you have ever noticed when you read online articles or blogs, a lot of the sentences are spaced out. This is intentional because research has shown that people are more inclined to read an article all the way to the end if their eyes only have to concentrate on small sections at a time. This can also be said with videos and having pattern interrupts (such as animated text and pictures popping in and out) rather than just being talking-head for the entire duration of the video.

And finally, consider including your digital signature at the end of your essay. This makes it look more professional.

Have Several Versions of Your Essay

Many scholarships have essays that have the same prompt, but with different word count requirements. So, it helps to already have several versions of basically the same essay saved in one document:

- 250, 500, 750, 1000 words, etc.

Also, make sure that each time you use that essay for a different scholarship, that you include somewhere at the end addressing the actual name of the scholarship (so that it sounds more personalized).

Example from my essay:

- "If awarded the *insert name of scholarship* this would have such a profound impact on my academic and career endeavors."

However, note when mentioning the name for that specific scholarship, that you omit that part for future applications. You don't want it to look obvious that you copied and pasted your essay but forgot to leave out the name of the scholarship you previously applied for! So, consider having within the **template** version of your essay **highlighted** where to insert the name.

As mentioned earlier in the book, if you are reusing your scholarship essay for other applications, try to look over it before sending it to ensure that the writing is up-to-date. Let's say that you suddenly accomplish or experience something huge — if so, make sure to incorporate that into your essay. Also, if you have a sentence that starts off as "Currently I am a ____" but that is no longer your situation, put that in the **past tense.**

Extra Writing Tips

If you still have time left over until the deadline — after writing your essay, step away from it for a couple of hours, or even several days — then read aloud and proofread your essay with fresh eyes. You might notice some things that need editing!

Also, get someone else to read it with HONEST feedback on what parts could be written better.

- Someone with a strong understanding of grammar, structure, and persuasive writing style.

Avoid repetitive wording as much as possible — use an online thesaurus by Googling synonyms for certain words to use in your essay.

Also, for me, when I read out loud my scholarship essay with a British/English accent — I write better and use fancier sentence structure and vocabulary. Try it, it may help you!

Find your ideal writing time. For me, I do my best writing late at night or near the deadline — I get a rush from writing last minute. (Don't be like me doing this — it's risky!)

The very first scholarship essay I wrote back in high school made the scholarship committee cry. If your essay can evoke some type of emotion — whether that's sentimental and/or motivational (rather than just reading like a resume) you're more likely to win — like I did. Your essay should be memorable.

When writing your essay, the goal is to speak from your heart. If you don't feel emotionally connected to what you just wrote — **keep writing** until you do.

If you have other people to read your essay before you submit it and they didn't feel moved in any type of way — or perhaps if they were in the shoes of those evaluating your essay and don't think they would give you the scholarship based on what you have written so far — **keep writing.**

Watch motivational speakers like Ted Talks to get an idea of what strong and impressionable language sounds like.

Ask yourself — "What is the most important part of my essay?"

Asking yourself this question will also help you with:

- Narrowing down what parts of your essay are essential to keep no matter the word count.
- What parts you can omit occasionally if you are applying for a scholarship that requires a shorter essay.
- Have these elements of your essay ranked from most important to least important to better navigate this.

Also, watch videos from YouTubers who read their college admissions or scholarship essays. I have seen quite a few students who got accepted into Ivy League schools do so.

And as a reminder, I already have two videos up on my YouTube channel where I read to the full extent my winning essays from Future and Floyd Mayweather.

- **Future essay:**
  www.youtube.com/watch?v=orQVEmI8CTA&t=354s
- **Floyd Mayweather essay:**
  www.youtube.com/watch?v=uqkb8jXon2M

Helpful Articles For Essay Writing

How To Write Scholarship Essays

    https://bit.ly/3gd3GK4

15 Expert Tips on How to Win College Scholarships

    https://bit.ly/3i5DJHZ

5 Ways to Make Your Scholarship Essay Stand Out

    https://bit.ly/3g6m5YP

Top 10 Tips for Writing Effective Scholarship Essays

    https://bit.ly/3g3TjIo

Why I Deserve This Scholarship Essay Examples

    https://bit.ly/3g0NivW

How to Write a Scholarship Essay Introduction (With Example)

    https://bit.ly/2EbHt1C

Persuasive Essay Using Ethos Pathos and Logos

    https://bit.ly/3i6sxuy

14 Scholarship Essay Examples That Won Thousands

    https://bit.ly/3hcQRRi

Part 4

Filling Out The Application

Free Online Resources and Reference Letters

Top Free Online Resources For Scholarship Applications

When editing and filling out PDF scholarship applications, use www.PDFescape.com — it's free!

If you have a MAC you can edit PDFs pretty well from there using the "Preview" software/application.

If you have anything that needs to go from a PDF to an image, or vice versa — or you need to split, compress, or combine several PDFs into one, then use these websites:

- https://combinepdf.com
- https://www.ilovepdf.com/split_pdf
- https://shrinkpdf.com/

Some scholarships might require a video instead of an essay, and these scholarships typically have a file-size limit/max of 100 MB. https://www.onlineconverter.com/compress-video can compress your video, with a minimal amount taken away from the actual video quality.

Some scholarships, internships, or jobs require you to submit your resume. Use www.ZipJob.com/free-review to get a free review/critique of your resume. Also, **use my resume template** that includes tips on standing out: https://bit.ly/3hCbB82

You may have a scholarship that requires a digital signature. Use the website www.mylivesignature.com/create-signature-step1 to create yours, pick the largest signature option, download it as a TRANSPARENT image, and paste it to any of your applications and scholarship essays.

Create a website/portfolio for free using www.Sites.Google.com

Use www.Canva.com to create your cover letter + resume. Canva allows you to create several versions of whatever you are trying to create (such as variants of your resume). It can be accessed online anywhere you go as long as you log in. The site also has templates for these things. Also, make sure your resume and cover letter are visually compelling – especially if you are studying something that is very dependent on visual presentation (such as media arts, graphics design, etc). Use black and white as the standard, but it doesn't hurt to add one or two other colors to make your resume stand out from others.

Consider trying Canva's pro version. I used this to create the visuals for my **scholarship online course,** which is much more extensive and detailed than this book. Go to the link below to watch the intro video: scholarship-guru.teachable.com

This next resource is more so for the college admissions process, which still ties back to being able to apply for a school's scholarships. It's called the commonapp.org. I would highly recommend using the Common App if you are still trying to figure out which school you want to go to. As mentioned earlier in this book, the more schools you apply for, the more likely you will be awarded at some point a school offering more money in scholarships – if not a full-ride.

There is also the commonblackcollegeapp.com which can be used to apply for many historically Black schools (HBCUs) all at the same time. The student I mentioned earlier who won over $459,000 in scholarships, used this resource. This site has a one-time $35 fee which is cheap considering that you can apply for multiple schools all at the same time.

Also, consider using similar sites to this, such as how I live in Texas and over here www.ApplyTexas.org is used for students to be able to apply for a mass amount of Texas universities with the same application. I used this when I was in high school.

So use these applications if you are still in the phase of looking for schools. They will save you so much time and will relieve some of the stress!

The scholarship process is very tedious. And the school admissions process is perhaps even more. It can especially be even more stressful if you perhaps are a first-generation student and you don't have any guidance from your parents or even resources provided by your school.

So many times I have heard from those I have helped win that they had to do everything by themselves and if they were offered scholarship assistance — the advice was too general to the point where it didn't help them win. I hope that so far through reading this book that the odds are more in your favor.

Another Way To Fill Out Online PDF Applications

Let's say that you are applying for the scholarship I won from the Broadcast Education Association.

For this award, you would have to fill out this application (https://bit.ly/2E7REVg) that is already optimized for being able to fill the needed information in with text boxes.

There is a way to edit the scholarship application in a new tab on your computer instead of using external sites or applications to complete it.

This might be a better alternative if your application has sensitive info and you don't trust external sites.

All you have to do is this step-by-step as seen in the link below:

https://rb.gy/va4jdq

Make sure to do this properly because without it you are very likely to export your filled-out application the wrong way and you will have to start all over from the very beginning because nothing was saved!

Trust me — don't make the same mistake I did so many times.

Reference/Recommendation Letters

Just like with any other component of your scholarship application, you must be organized — especially with this.

Download the template (https://rb.gy/fnxhqf) of a brag letter. This will help those writing a reference letter for you have a more outlined idea of what to write.

Have several reference letters already ready to go.

- Scholarships that require reference aka recommendation letters typically will need two to three letters.

Make sure your letters don't sound the same!

Sometimes getting these letters from only educators will have basically the same writing style. It helps that they vary in writing style, length, and who's writing it such as from a:

- Professor, classmate, employer, organization member etc.
  - This makes you seem more 'well-rounded'.

Your reference letters should **humanize** your overall application and reiterate your work ethic.

Another tip is to use signatures and official letterheads. They make letters seem more trustworthy/professional.

Also, make sure that your letters of recommendation can back up the claims made in your scholarship essay; however, at the same time, they shouldn't just be carbon copies of what you already wrote there. They should offer a different perspective and also highlight how you were able to overcome a challenge.

Example Of Reference/ Recommendation Letter

Mayborn School of Journalism
OFFICE OF THE DEAN

October 7, 2019

To the scholarship committee representing PILOT Media Technology and Innovation:

Thank you for the opportunity to endorse Carlynn Greene as a candidate for your scholarship. Although I have only known Carlynn for a year – a period that includes collaboration in the classroom – I am honored that she asked me to recommend her.

██

junior year. I can't think of a harder working student and I know she would be a great representative of the PILOT Media Technology and Innovation Scholarship.

Please do not hesitate to contact me to hear more about this exceptional, young journalist.

My best,

Jasmine C. Johnson

Mayborn Scholar/Graduate Student
University of North Texas
jasmine█████████xas.edu
4█████████

Key Components Of Reference/ Recommendation Letter

- Dated: month-date-year (Example: July 21, 2020)
    - Other countries will have the date mentioned first.
- Official letterhead from establishment
    - You can find this by searching online via Google Images or by going to that scholarship's website
    - An alternative way would be to copy/paste or screenshot from existing letters you may have access to
        - **NOTE**: Make sure it isn't pixelated / blurry!
- Addresses the name of the foundation / organization and the name of the scholarship in the first sentence
    - Or can start with, "To whom it may concern ..."
- Mentions the name of the scholarship
    - Place in last or second to last paragraph
- Print name + digital signature
- Contact (email, phone number, website, mailing etc.)

NOTE: The previous page is a letter from a graduate student classmate. Don't think that the letters are only acceptable from teachers, professors, or your employer. Your friend, family, coworker, or classmate may just know you and your work ethic more and have more to say to make your application stand out more than your educators or boss!

So to sum it all up, have a minimum of two letters:

- One that establishes your credibility and professionalism
    - Typically from an educator, boss, etc.
- One that establishes your character and work ethic
    - Typically from a friend, coworker, classmate, etc.

Get Permission To Modify Recommendation Letters

With me, I applied for a lot of scholarships (100+), and the majority of them required letters. **However,** it would become awfully redundant if I were to email my teachers, mentors, classmates, etc., every time I needed them to write a letter that's written out specifically to whatever scholarship committee. That might annoy them, or worse my email requests for yet another letter would just be ignored or left on read.

So, what I do instead — with the permission of the original writer of course — is edit a few things here and there.

NOTE: I don't change the actual content of the letter regarding what they are saying about me. With that being said, **do not change the actual content** of your letters because **that would be unethical.** Plus, with these recommendation letters, sometimes those evaluating will contact those people to see if what they wrote matches up. If it doesn't, that would be a red flag to them and as a result, your scholarship application won't be taken into consideration.

There are also applications that have the option of submitting **"blind recommendations"** meaning ones that those writing your letters have to personally submit to an online portal rather than you submitting them. Some scholarships or colleges for admissions **may favor** someone with blind letters over one with letters they attached themselves because they find them more credible.

How To Modify Reference Letters

I only change:

- To who the letter is being written out to
- The date it was written (so that the letter doesn't look outdated but more current)
- Insert the name of the scholarship I am applying for and who it is addressed to. **For example:**
  - Scholarship name — I Am A Dreamer Scholarship
  - Addressed to — Future's Freewishes Foundation

Example: "I am highly recommending Carlynn Greene to the I Am A Dreamer Scholarship through Future's Freewishes Foundation."

I also modify my letters of recommendation for job applications. Also, if whoever wrote the essay forgot to put an official letter header, contact info, etc. — I add that.

If there are typos or weird grammar — because not every person has perfect writing skills — then I proofread/edit that as well. Then after doing all that, when it's time to send the completed application, I also send the person of reference the edited version of their letter.

Another thing you can modify regarding the audience is when you are transforming a scholarship reference letter to a job reference letter (or vice versa). For instance, if there was a job I applied for and a sentence in the letter said "I highly recommend them for this job position" that sentence would not make sense for a scholarship application. So you would change it to "I highly recommend them for this scholarship."

The Ideal People For Reference Letters

Letters of reference/recommendation are like an extension of your scholarship essay. And just as how your essay is the 'heart' of your application, you should think of the letters as being the 'liver'. You can still live with only one part of a liver (one reference letter), but the more parts there are (the more reference letters), the stronger you are (the stronger your application is).

So, choose wisely who will do the letters based on these criteria:

- Someone who knows you well enough
- Who writes well enough
- Who has great time management and commits to deadlines
- Who is easy to contact via not just email, but also via their phone and/or social media (because they may not check their email often or get bombarded with too many and yours might get lost along the way)

And again, send out several reminders to those writing your letters when it nears the deadline!

It might even help for you to **give them a fake deadline,** just as how I advised doing so earlier in the book when creating your master list of scholarships.

You might be a procrastinator, however they might just be too.

Overall Winning Application

This is a broadcasting scholarship that I won for $1,000 linked here: https://rb.gy/dbgo4g

Use www.combinepdf.com to combine all elements required such as:

- Application
- Essay
- Recommendation letters
- Cover Letter
- Resume
- Unofficial or official transcript
- Proof of Enrollment
  - Example: from the National Clearing House

Try and make sure that the elements required for your application are in the order of which they are listed/mentioned on the criteria part of the application.

Triple-check that you have all the components required.

Make sure there are no typos in your essay(s), resume, cover letter — and especially your contact info as well as the contact info of those you have indicated as your references.

If you feel like it and want to show off some graphic design skills, you can create a cover page for your application with:

- The name of the scholarship + their logo
- Your name
- The date of submission

More Tips

If you see a scholarship that you qualify for, but you missed the deadline, still, make an effort to bookmark or keep it listed somewhere so that you can apply for it when it opens again.

Most scholarship committees prefer for applications to be electronically sent in and filled in digitally rather than sent in the mail or handwritten.

Make sure to check your mailbox and email regularly. Sometimes your scholarship might accidentally be sent to the wrong physical mailbox or filtered to spam/junk email — happened to me for two different scholarships I won. I nearly wasn't awarded because of it. So, watch out!

Apply for scholarships relating to your minor(s).

Keep applying! Set a goal for yourself and search and apply for at least one scholarship a day or 5-10 within a week.

Make sure your social media is clean! The last thing you want is to have your scholarship taken away because of something problematic. And if it isn't clean — set your account to private and make a professional account that's public because some scholarships require links to your social media.

Read other people's winning scholarship essays. You can always refer back to how I write mine, but that isn't the only way to win. There are different styles that might resonate with you more and be able to capture what you are trying to come across within your writing.

For the scholarship I won from Floyd Mayweather, I was able to find that after going to the eighth page of a Google search. So with that being said, when looking up scholarships, don't limit yourself to just the first one or two pages of results. Keep going!

If you are someone who has already been awarded a considerable amount of money in financial aid, there may be a part on the application that says, "Please state other outside financial awards you have received."

In this part, you don't want to seem as if you got too much money, because then they'll think you don't need any more money. However, you still do need money because that's why you're applying for that scholarship in the first place!

Instead, try to only mention maybe two or three that you have been awarded in scholarships, and perhaps one or two that you have been awarded in grants.

For additional tips and scholarship alerts, join the **discord group chat!** It really does help to be a part of a community. I remember **how alone I felt** going through the scholarship process — especially when I would receive rejection letters. Plus, those in the chat might just have advice and suggested scholarships that work better for you since they more closely relate to your background/demographic.

- https://discord.gg/dUtaBEZYVc

Video Submission Scholarships

Some scholarships require you to submit a video of yourself detailing who you are and why you deserve to be awarded the scholarship. Video submission scholarships might want you to link a YouTube URL, whereas others might want you to attach the video file as a .MP4. Many video scholarships have a max file size of 100 megabytes (MB).

So consider using www.onlineconverter.com/compress-video to compress your video file size to less than 100 MB.

For an example of what a winning scholarship video can look like, view this one from a student who bought this book and watched my YouTube videos who was able to win **$100,000 from Dr. Pepper's Tuition Giveaway:** https://youtu.be/ffIn6ouotog Some **key takeaways** as seen from his scholarship video are to:

- Introduce yourself (your name, major, where you study)
- Have images/video clips in sync with narration
- Use non-copyrighted/license-free/royalty-free music
- Address your audience on how the scholarship will help you ("Dr. Pepper, if you were to award me ...")
- Stay in theme (in the video he wears a Dr. Pepper shirt and drinks Dr. Pepper during the art timelapse)

If you perhaps are not good with filming or video editing, then have someone else to do so for you. Also, make sure that your lighting is consistent (evenly lighting your face and not over or underexposed) and that the audio isn't raspy, low, or too high and grainy. There are **so many technical elements** that go into creating a great video-based scholarship submission and I go much more into detail about this in my **online course.**

84

Acing Scholarship Interviews

Some scholarships have interviews to finalize who wins. These interviews can be in person or virtually, such as via Zoom.

With over 86,000+ views, my YouTube video on how to ace scholarship interviews has helped a lot of students in the comment section win their scholarships! Some even managed to get full-ride scholarships thanks to the advice in it! **Link here:** https://www.youtube.com/watch?v=r18shWM3Qqo

This video covers everything you need to know — from how to dress to what to say. Also, if you find yourself having to do a **virtual interview**, then follow these quick tips:

Appearance — Dress professionally and wear some makeup.

Setting — Minimize distractions in the background; no swivel chairs, moving ceiling fans, people, and evenly light your face.

Technical — Test your audio and visual equipment with others before your interview and silence your phone's notifications.

Another tip is to do research before the interview about not only that establishment giving out the scholarship, but if accessible, also who will be judging you and their background.

Also, my **online course** offers **exclusive** and even more comprehensive lessons outside of this book and my YouTube channel. So, consider enrolling! The master course is basically a bundle of all my services together. It comes with this book, essay editing, application reviewing, interview coaching, and personalized advising via Zoom. **Link**: https://bit.ly/2EsnRXx

My Services/Products

Master list of all URLs mentioned in book: https://bit.ly/TSAurls

(Or **scan the QR code** below to access all the links that were mentioned in this book on one Google document!)

Scholarships I give out (as a reminder, part of the sales from this book goes towards giving out scholarships to others):

https://bit.ly/scholarshipsSG

Website: https://www.scholarship-guru.com/

Scholarship online course: scholarship-guru.teachable.com/

Scholarship application review service: https://bit.ly/36ewPDl

The Scholarship Algorithm book paywall: bit.ly/TSAbook

Scholarship Advising (two options below)

> **Free group chat:** https://discord.gg/dUtaBEZYVc

> **Personalized 1-on-1 advising:** https://bit.ly/3kzXGNY

Scholarship essay editing: https://bit.ly/2FMfBCt

Download FREE PDF of the essay tips: https://adobe.ly/3cMi4aJ

My YouTube channel https://bit.ly/espdaniellaplaylist

Differences between YouTube, book, and online course:

https://bit.ly/36oMVA9

Spread The Word & Share

Do you know other students, parents, or educators looking for scholarships? Then, let them know about my social media videos, this book, online course, and personalized scholarship services!

Also, would you like for me to speak and teach my scholarship master class (which is a 1-hour mini-version from my **online course / program**) to your school, organization, or event?

Then, **share** (*via text, social media, verbally etc.,*) with others the two links below for more information:
Services/products listed on my website:

https://beacons.ai/scholarshipguru/services

Sign up page for speaking engagement

https://scholarshipguru-speaking.my.canva.site/

Nominate Me For Ted-Talk

This book — although very detailed — is only a snippet of what I know about scholarships.

Once again, the **online course** is much more extensive/detailed and analyzes more in-depth my techniques as seen from my winning scholarship applications.

I want to bring the knowledge that I have about scholarships to the global stage. **Here's how you can help me get there:**

Go to the link below to nominate me! It details what to mention in my nomination.

https://bit.ly/2ZXEEt1

Send the link above out to others. The more nominations, the more likely this can become a reality!

Press coverage about me:

Broadcasted live interview Fox 5 News Washington, D.C
www.fox5dc.com/video/930533

Broadcasted video story from Fox 4 News https://bit.ly/2Eccn9Y

Article from Denton Record-Chronicle https://bit.ly/3kUwiuX

Contact / Socials

Email: GreeneCarlynn@gmail.com

TikTok & YouTube: @ESPDaniella

Instagram: @Carle100

Twitter and LinkedIn: @CarlynnGreene

Facebook: @CarlynnDG

Click the link below to view **testimonies** from those who won!

https://bit.ly/SGscholarshipwinners

The Sequel To This Book

When it comes to scholarships, they are somewhat dependent on your academics and what you are involved in while at school. Having these elements will increase your chances of winning.

If you want to learn all my techniques to getting a 4.0 GPA from high school to college (despite barely studying, yet retaining information in less time), how I was able to secure multiple all-expenses-paid internships and other opportunities with financial benefits — then consider getting my other book:

School Code

Link here: https://carlynn.ck.page/products/school-code-ebook

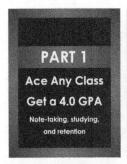

The reason I'm passing." - *Mazlin, college student, law school*

"Carlynn always gives out the best school advice. No wonder she made it to the news. She's always willing to help others and offer support." - *Ivy*

THIS BOOK IS BROKEN UP IN FOUR PARTS:

1 ACE ANY CLASS, GET A 4.0 GPA

From the time of high school through college, I've always managed to get a 4.0 GPA. However, it may come as surprise that I am actually not very studious and tend to procrastinate. In this section, you will learn my study hacks and how I retain info in less time using unorthodox methods.

2 COMMUNICATION X NETWORKING

This part covers how you can finesse your way into opportunities while in school. You don't necessarily have to be very sociable or extroverted to get ahead. Sometimes, less is more and being intentional with every word and conversation by learning / practicing strategic communication skills.

3 MENTAL HEALTH X HAPPINESS

Mental health is very important and can either positively or negatively affect your academic performance and overall life. This chapter covers how you can stay in the best of spirits while in school, such as through self-therapy practices, motivational content, exercises, and much more.

4 SAVE MONEY, MAKE MONEY

Many know me as the 'Scholarship Guru' having helped students win scholarships for school. This book covers some tips regarding scholarships as well how to save money on school and living expenses, side-hustles you can start, and how to get internships, part-time jobs, and your dream job.

CARLYNN D. GREENE

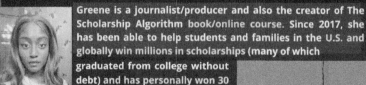

Greene is a journalist/producer and also the creator of The Scholarship Algorithm book/online course. Since 2017, she has been able to help students and families in the U.S. and globally win millions in scholarships (many of which graduated from college without debt) and has personally won 30 awards, totaling at $125,000.

She aspires to propose legislation for additional student financial aid, and to tour across the U.S. teaching her scholarship masterclass at schools, nonprofit events, and conferences.

"What you need to know to be successful in high school and college."

SCHOOL CODE

CARLYNN D. GREENE

Made in the USA
Monee, IL
07 November 2024

69567481R00069